LETTERS FROM CICELY

**A collection of Cicely Sponge's
nonsensical letters
to the Bavard Bar**

TIM B'VARD

Illustrated by Maria O'Neill

Letters from Cicely

Copyright © 2024 by Tim B'vard

Published by The Bavard Bar - www.bavardbar.co.uk

All rights reserved.

No part of this book may be reproduced or transmitted in any form without the author's permission, except for brief quotations in reviews.

This is a work of fiction. As such, any references to real people, living or dead, companies, organisations or actual events are made up and entirely fictional. For example, as far as Cicely knows, Tom Cruise doesn't have a Ferret and Fungi Farm in East Midlothian, and nor does Dame Judi Dench have a Line Dancing themed Ski Jump and Apple Bobbing Centre. Whether either of them has plans to develop such facilities in the future is also unknown to Cicely.

First published in the United Kingdom in December 2024.

ISBN: 978-1-0685477-6-8

Book Cover and Interior design by Printing Direct
printingdirect.com

Illustrations by Maria O'Neill ⊙ @mariaoneillart

Edited by Laurine Waille, the fabulous editor.

For permissions and queries or to contact the author, please email tim@bavardbar.co.uk

DEDICATION

This book is dedicated to my Bhodisattva,
Julia Chi Taylor, without whose guidance Cicely is unlikely to
have emerged. It is also dedicated to my beautiful daughter,
Hannah, with a heartfelt wish that her life is filled with
joyous nonsense and infinite love. Finally, it is dedicated to
my beautiful girlfriend and fabulous editor,
Laurine Waille, and my wonderful friend, Susie Barnard.

IN MEMORIAM

Poppy the dog, who died on 21 March 2024, aged 14 1/2 years. She was a wonderful companion and lived a wonderful life.

It's all nonsense

CONTENTS

Foreword	10
Introduction	11
HOLIDAYS & TRAVEL	15
TV & ENTERTAINMENT	21
FOOD & DRINK	27
SPORT & LEISURE	38
HOBBIES & PASTIMES	47
PHILOSOPHY & SPIRITUALITY	57
MUSIC	69
WORK & MONEY	79
Acknowledgements	85
About the Author	89
About the Artist	91

FOREWORD

This foreword is not written by Sir David Attenborough. Nor is it written by Miriam Margolyes, Stephen Fry, Sandi Toksvig, David Walliams or Dame Maureen Lipman. There are many possible reasons for this, one of which could be that I never asked them.

It's also not written by Jamie Oliver or Delia Smith. Possibly because it's not a cookbook.

December 2024
St Leonards-on-Sea

INTRODUCTION

Who is Cicely Sponge? Well, according to her bio on the Bavard Bar website, she's a former flamenco dancer living in a slightly damp two-bedroom maisonette in Polegate with her long-term friend Alfredo (an Italian downhill skier) and a quintet of budgerigars. She's in the autumn of her days and enjoys the occasional pint of stout, pickled eggs, and a good old-fashioned arm wrestle. She also quite likes sea fishing.

But what is the Bavard Bar? And why does Cicely write to it relentlessly?

I opened the Bavard Bar show in March 2017 at Printers Playhouse in Eastbourne, followed in May 2017 at Kino-Teatr in St Leonards-on-Sea. Bavard comes from the French verb 'bavarder', meaning to chat, and the show started as a talk show, where three regular people take the stage and share something they're passionate about for around 15 minutes each. An everyman's TED talks if you like, although it quickly developed into much more than a night of talks.

Having grown up on a love of comedy, in particular nonsense, surreal and absurdist humour, I started to develop comedy games that the audience could participate in on the night if they wished. My warmup introductions to each show also became more silly and standup than anything else, and it wasn't long before the Bavard Bar became a monthly fixture at both venues in both towns.

The games I introduced, such as the KP Lite, Oojah Kappivvy and Bohemia Road, became regular staples. People enjoyed them alongside the unique, extraordinary and often unusual passions that the speakers, or bavarders as they became known, shared.

In late 2019, I moved the Eastbourne show from Printers Playhouse to Towner. In the intervening years, I added new audience games, including Victoria Drive, Make It Stop, and Pearl Or Dean, plus a caption competition for the audience to muse on throughout the evening. Woven through the nights, my Piano Man, Dan, played songs in the intervals inspired by the speakers' passions, and artist Maria O'Neill sat in the audience, drawing each speaker in the half-light of each dimly lit theatre.

That's how the show developed and is still developing. Wonderfully, the show has proved very popular with the discerning public of St Leonards, Hastings, and Eastbourne. Thanks to Simon Charterton, it even has an 'Avant Bavard', when his band, Simon&thePope, plays live music before every show at Kino-Teatr.

So, where does Cicely come in?

In the mid to late 1970s, BBC Radio 4 ran a comedy series called The Burkiss Way. I was a little too young to hear it the first time around. However, on my dad's recommendation, a fellow lover of nonsense and the absurd, I caught the repeats in the 1980s just as I was reaching my teens. I was hooked. I recorded each episode on one side of a TDK 90 and built up a stack. Around the same time, I discovered shows like 'I'm Sorry I'll Read That Again' ('ISIRTA') and 'Radio Active' and filled up yet more TDK 90s.

One of the key things those shows had in common was a large amount of nonsense. As well as absurdist characters, such as Eric Pode from Croydon and Lady Constance de Coverlet. Later in life, along with many readers, no doubt, I enjoyed the musings of Mrs Trellis from North Wales and her regular letters to Humphrey Littleton and Jack Dee on 'I'm Sorry I Haven't A Clue', an iteration of ISIRTA.

Having driven between Hastings and Eastbourne countless times over the years, I was aware of the small town of Polegate. Aware of it, but I rarely visited it, as it had been long ago by-passed. But I was struck by its name, which I found, for no particular reason, joyfully absurd.

Somehow and entirely unconsciously, this confusion of sources coalesced in my mind in late 2018. In October of that year, I had a show at Kino-Teatr where one of the bavarders, Andy Spector, gave a brilliant 'bavard' about 'How to become a Meteorite Hunter'. It was a fascinating talk, with a lot of nonsense and absurdism, though not too much to detract from the subject.

Shortly after that talk, Cicely Sponge wrote me her first letter:

Dear Mr Bar,

I went to the Bavard Bar last Wednesday and was highly disturbed. Not only did you have someone talking about Meteorites, a subject in which I have no interest, but no one spoke about azaleas. Why?

Yours, Cicely Sponge, Polegate

Cicely was born.

Since her first letter in October 2018, Cicely has written me over 150 letters, sharing her invaluable views and experiences on a wide range of subjects, including Philosophy, Spirituality, Sport, Travel, and Food and Drink, to name just a few. I have never replied to one of Cicely's letters, but that has never stopped her writing. If anything, it's quite possibly only encouraged her to write more.

I hope you enjoy reading Cicely's letters as much as she enjoyed writing them.

HOLIDAYS & TRAVEL

August 2024
Dear Mr Bar,

I've just returned from a camping holiday in the English countryside. The best thing about the holiday was waking up in my own bed this morning and realising I was no longer camping. Coupled with the fact that visiting my bathroom now feels like a mini-break at a wellness centre.

Yours, Cicely Sponge, Polegate

June 2024
Dear Mr Bar,

Some people think 'hope springs eternal'. Maybe, but I doubt those people have experienced a fortnight's family caravanning holiday in Skegness.

Yours, Cicely Sponge, Polegate

June 2024

Dear Mr Bar,

If you're not going on holiday, you can always make people think you're going on holiday by walking around all day holding your passport and pulling one of those suitcases on wheels. Not only will people wish you a great time, you won't have to go through security.

Yours, Cicely Sponge, Polegate

August 2023

Dear Mr Bar,

I had planned to go camping this summer. Instead, I spent a week sleeping in my kitchen with the windows open and the taps running. I've had the same experience and saved a fortune on camping fees. I'd recommend it.

Yours, Cicely Sponge, Polegate

June 2023
Dear Mr Bar,

I love the summer as much as the next octogenarian, but finding myself newly single, I'm struggling to apply my Hawaiian Tropic. If you could spare a minute, I'm on the beach next to Groyne 47.

Yours, Cicely Sponge, Polegate

January 2021
Dear Mr Bar,

I've just heard that the people of Sidley have voted to leave Rother and set up a Municipality similar to Monaco. Only with fewer yachts. Would you like to go halves on a timeshare there with me?

Yours, Cicely Sponge, Polegate

August 2020
Dear Mr Bar,

If there's a badger in your bed, you're probably camping.

Yours, Cicely Sponge, Polegate

January 2020
Dear Mr Bar,

I've just booked my summer holiday. Two weeks in East Croydon may not be everyone's first choice, but if you want to avoid tourists, you may want to consider it.

Yours, Cicely Sponge, Polegate

July 2019
Dear Mr Bar,

Given the heat, I'm considering my wardrobe for your August Bavards. Is there a Bavardian dress code, or will Crocs and a Pashmina be acceptable?

Yours, Cicely Sponge, Polegate

TV & ENTERTAINMENT

August 2024
Dear Mr Bar,

As Chairman of The Polegate & Aberfeldy Tap Dancing and Fermented Food Society, I'm organising our annual festival. We invited Benedict Cumberbatch to open the festival since he's an avid tap dancer and keen amateur fermenter. Disappointingly, he declined, but he has sent us a pair of his tap dancing shoes and a partially fermented cauliflower. We'll raffle the tap dancing shoes, but if you'd like Benedict's semi-fermented cauliflower, drop me a line.

Yours, Cicely Sponge, Polegate

March 2024
Dear Mr Bar,

I toured with Keith Harris and Orville in the 1980s and remember, with fondness, tinged with some embarrassment, the night we spent in a launderette in Lowestoft. Fondness because it was Keith's birthday. Embarrassment because I inadvertently tumble-dried Orville, and he was never really the same again.

Yours,
Cicely Sponge,
Polegate

August 2023
Dear Mr Bar,

It's nice to see Harrison Ford back on the big screen. I spent much of the '80s playing his stunt double – at Canasta.

Yours, Cicely Sponge, Polegate

October 2022

Dear Mr Bar,

I've been offered the part of James Bond in the next Bond movie, 'No One Ever Dies,' in which 007 identifies as a woman. I still save the world but with no loss of life or property damage.

Yours, Cicely Sponge, Polegate

August 2022

Dear Mr Bar,

It's the annual awayday of the Sidley & Dunstable Society of Mandolin Tuners and Clay Pigeon Fanciers. We spent the morning foraging on Tom Cruise's East Midlothian Ferret and Fungi Farm, and the afternoon in A&E. Join us next year when we're planning a trip to Dame Judi Dench's Line Dancing themed Ski Jump and Apple Bobbing Centre.

Yours, Cicely Sponge, Polegate

October 2021

Dear Mr Bar,

Do you know who is responsible for Tupperware Parties? Only I've got a cupboard full of lids I need to return.

Yours, Cicely Sponge, Polegate

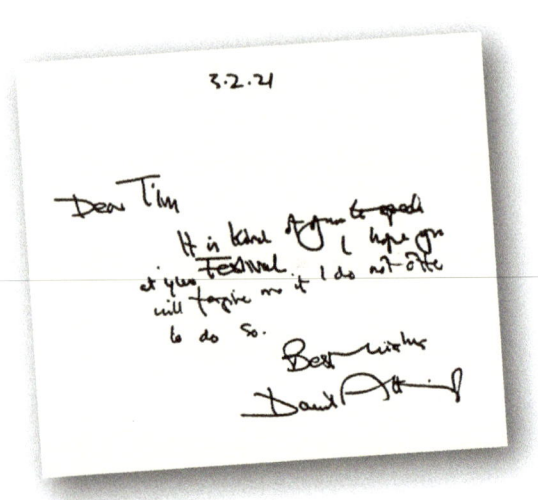

March 2021
Dear Mr Bar,

Inspired by Sir David Attenborough, please put me down as not speaking at your Bavard Bar in April. I look forward to it.

Yours, Cicely Sponge, Polegate

May 2020
Dear Mr Bar,

Congratulations on reaching the third anniversary of your show. I remember celebrating the third anniversary of Polegate's Free Diving Society. Eamonn Holmes had been due to attend, but sadly he took a wrong turn off the A259 and ended up hosting Polegate's 17th Torchlight Wheelbarrow procession.

Yours, Cicely Sponge, Polegate

March 2020

Dear Mr Bar,

On this day in 1971, I spent a glorious afternoon riding pillion for Peter Purves as a stunt double for Valerie Singleton. The piece never aired, as Peter crashed into a horse-drawn chariot driven by Lionel Blair rehearsing for 'Ben-Hur the Musical' on the B4388 just outside Welshpool.

Yours, Cicely Sponge, Polegate

July 2019

Dear Mr Bar,

Having been glued to the TV set all day Sunday, I was relieved to have it removed by a surgeon earlier today. My hands may now be gloved, but I'll be at Wednesday's Bavard Bar for sure!

Yours, Cicely Sponge, Polegate

June 2019

Dear Mr Bar,

I had to withdraw from this year's Love Island as I had a recurrence of gout. I've taken solace in my subscription to 'Linoleum Monthly' and look forward to bavarding soon on a variety of surfaces.

Yours, Cicely Sponge, Polegate

May 2019
Dear Mr Bar,

As you know, I turned down the role of Sandy in Grease to pursue my vocation as a seafaring clairvoyant. Whilst that didn't work out, I do have some stories from my time working on board the Canvey Island ferry in the late '70s. I'd be happy to 'bavard' about them.

Yours, Cicely Sponge, Polegate

February 2019
Dear Mr Bar,

As a long-standing fan of Baywatch, I heard a rumour that The Hoff is bavarding at Wednesday's show. Supported by Rick Astley on kazoo, with a tap dancing finale performed by the entire cast of Neighbours from 1991. Could this be true?

Yours, Cicely Sponge, Polegate

FOOD & DRINK

October 2024

Dear Mr Bar,

I'm becoming increasingly frustrated by theatres serving ice cream in the interval. When did they serve the main course? Surely a simple chicken teriyaki on a bed of saffron noodles or a duck egg omelette infused with truffle oil wouldn't be too much to ask. They could save the ice cream for the end.

Yours, Cicely Sponge, Polegate

September 2024

Dear Mr Bar,

1972 was a difficult year for me as although I broke the world record for consuming the most prunes in the fastest time, I hadn't pitted them. The fallout from the resulting blockage required the attendance of more than one fire crew at my maisonette, an event that has lingered long in the annals of Polegate's renowned firefighting history.

Yours, Cicely Sponge, Polegate

July 2024

Dear Mr Bar,

I've long been a fan of scrambled eggs, but I've noticed young people barely talk about them. Any idea why?

Yours, Cicely Sponge, Polegate

May 2024
Dear Mr Bar,

I'm delighted to be able to tell you that finally, after countless submissions, my article on 'How to Pickle a Haddock' has been accepted by the UK's leading pickling journal, 'Beyond Rollmops'. Initially the editors felt the haddock was out of financial reach for most picklers. But as I explain in the article, if you can't afford a haddock, you'll achieve the same results by pickling your socks.

Yours, Cicely Sponge, Polegate

May 2024
Dear Mr Bar,

If, like me, you were a teenage trampoline sensation, the chances are you'll now be suffering from mild tinnitus. I'd recommend eating pork scratchings and hazelnuts mixed with boiled tofu. You may like to drizzle this dish with mayonnaise and marmite, or maymite, as I like to call it. It doesn't cure the tinnitus but you won't be aware you have the condition while you eat it.

Yours, Cicely Sponge, Polegate

April 2024
Dear Mr Bar,

Growing up in Nantwich in the 1970s, and as the only child of a fondue set and coffee percolator salesman, I'm understandably well accustomed to high-class living and fine dining. Which is why I find this recent trend by restaurants to state the kitchen utensils used to cook the food somewhat irksome. If I want a fried egg, there is no need for the restaurant to tell me it will be 'pan-fried'. As an adult human in possession of most of my teeth and with a part share in a semi-functional hot tub, I am reasonably able to discern that my egg is unlikely to be fried in a toaster.

Yours, Cicely Sponge, Polegate

February 2024
Dear Mr Bar,

As Chairman of Polegate's foremost Artichoke Appreciation Society, we've updated our motto to 'E pluribus unum artichoke'. Something else that sets us apart from Polegate's other Artichoke Appreciation Societies.

Yours, Cicely Sponge, Polegate

November 2023
Dear Mr Bar,

I'm having a clearout. I've got half a box of raspberry tea bags, a polyester sarong, and most of the second series of Lovejoy on VHS. I'm reluctant to let go of the sarong or Lovejoy, but if you take the tea bags, you can have the lot.

Yours, Cicely Sponge, Polegate

November 2023
Dear Mr Bar,

I went on a coach trip to Nantwich in 1982. Whilst there I ate at the A530 Café and had to choose between soup of the day (minestrone) and a jacket potato with cheese. I went for the soup and have regretted my decision ever since.

Yours, Cicely Sponge, Polegate

October 2023
Dear Mr Bar,

Would you object to me bringing a foot spa to Wednesday's show? Only I have a painful bunion, and Epsom salts are the only thing that gets me through the day. Well, that and a schooner of Harveys Bristol Cream.

Yours, Cicely Sponge, Polegate

October 2023
Dear Mr Bar,

While preparing my mid-morning omelette, Jesus' face appeared in the eggy mixture. Although it could have been Demis Roussos. Regardless, I'll never receive whatever message they had for me as I've decided to boil my eggs in future.

Yours, Cicely Sponge, Polegate

September 2023
Dear Mr Bar,

I'm often credited with inventing the internal combustion engine. This isn't true, but I did once make a lemon meringue pie.

Yours, Cicely Sponge, Polegate

September 2023
Dear Mr Bar,

I've just secured a place in Polegate's annual turnip tossing competition. Having only ever tossed swedes, I'm a bit of an underdog. But as Rick Stein famously said: "Nowt's the difference 'tween a turnip and a swede." And having built his culinary empire on root vegetables, he should know.

Yours, Cicely Sponge, Polegate

August 2023
Dear Mr Bar,

I've just embarked on the first-ever solo circumnavigation of Polegate in a pedalo dressed as Heston Blumenthal. It's an audacious undertaking and doesn't come without risk. But as Heston famously said: 'Don't put all your minestrone in one basket'. So I've packed a selection of soft cheeses, and with a fair wind, expect to be home by Autumn.

Yours, Cicely Sponge, Polegate

May 2023

Dear Mr Bar,

Since my partner, Alfredo, ran off with a long-distance Flamenco Dancer, I've been living on my own. I now enjoy a varied diet of ready meals for one. From Chocolate Hobnobs to Custard Creams, my meals are genuinely 'ready' straight out of the packet.

Yours, Cicely Sponge, Polegate

January 2023

Dear Mr Bar,

I have three Pigs and one Blanket left over from Christmas. Plus seven Sprouts. You're welcome to the lot if you can collect. I'd drop them off, but I'm bedridden due to a mystery bout of food poisoning.

Yours, Cicely Sponge, Polegate

July 2022

Dear Mr Bar,

Since my pelvic floor collapsed at 11:47 am on 27th March 2003, I have dedicated my life to rebuilding it. By committing to an exclusively offal-based diet and practising pilates 12 hours every day, I'm now strong enough downstairs to crack a Brazil nut. Never give up on your dreams, Mr Bar.

Yours, Cicely Sponge, Polegate

February 2022
Dear Mr Bar

I've always been partial to a boiled egg and a pickled herring, and I wondered whether you would consider serving them as interval snacks?

Yours, Cicely Sponge, Polegate

September 2021
Dear Mr Bar,

Now that we've 'taken back control', can you tell me where I can get a packet of Hobnobs and some thermal underwear? Within walking distance.

Yours, Cicely Sponge, Polegate

October 2021
Dear Mr Bar,

I have 17 Noel Edmonds shaped egg cups to give away. Noel was a huge inspiration to me and my hope is that my egg cups will enable future generations to continue being inspired by him. At least over breakfast.

Yours, Cicely Sponge, Polegate

November 2021
Dear Mr Bar,

As founder and only member of the Polegate and District Cheese Pickling Society, I am always on the lookout for new cheeses. And members. If you know anyone?

Yours, Cicely Sponge, Polegate

February 2020
Dear Mr Bar,

At a recent meeting of the Polegate Apple Bobbing and Thimble Twirling Society, a club steeped in controversy over its decision to cancel its 1988 summer awayday to Pevensey following the great 1988 apple and thimble shortage, I felt the decision to allow the use of 'alternative hard fruit such as pineapples' was a backward step that would only serve to further diminish our club's reputation.

Yours, Cicely Sponge, Polegate

October 2019
Dear Mr Bar,

I have developed a new passion and am keen to share it with your audience. Courgettes. I'll bring samples.

Yours, Cicely Sponge, Polegate

January 2020
Dear Mr Bar,

I wondered if you would be interested in attending the annual dinner dance of Polegate's Caving and Figure Skating Club. I have quite a lot of leftover turkey, and if you had any sprouts, we could make it a night to remember—or forget, depending on the state of your sprouts.

Yours, Cicely Sponge, Polegate

August 2019
Dear Mr Bar,

Given the craze of going 'out out', I thought I'd stay 'in in'. I've got seven litres of drinking chocolate, a KFC Bargain Bucket, and the entire back catalogue of 'Songs of Praise' on VHS. If that's not a stairway to heaven, I don't know what is.

Yours, Cicely Sponge, Polegate

April 2019
Dear Mr Bar,

I've recently returned from spending 28 years on a desert island just off the A27. I passed the time by inventing the internet and fine-tuning the recipe for Dairylea Triangles. Let me know if you're in need of a cheese and web-based talk and I'll happily step up.

Yours, Cicely Sponge, Polegate

January 2019
Dear Mr Bar,

Would you have any use for a heated oven glove? It's an unwanted gift as I have decided to exist on a diet of raw food for the first half of 2019. I don't expect to make it to the second half.

Yours, Cicely Sponge, Polegate

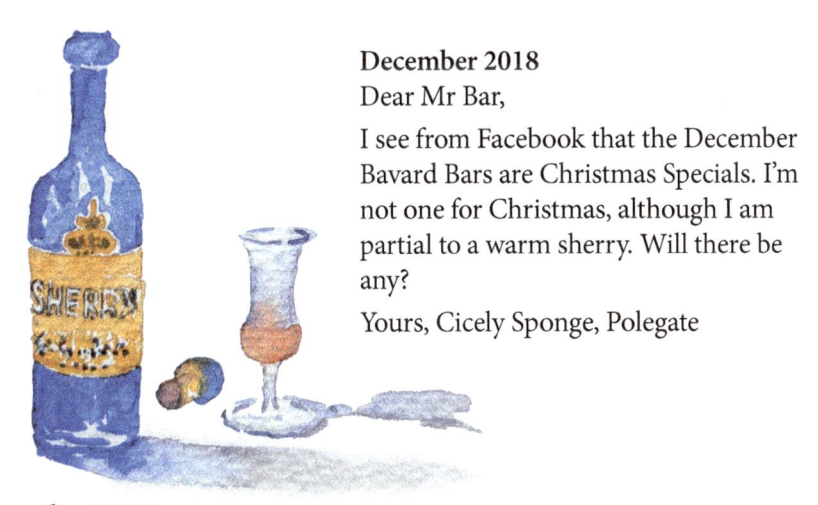

December 2018
Dear Mr Bar,

I see from Facebook that the December Bavard Bars are Christmas Specials. I'm not one for Christmas, although I am partial to a warm sherry. Will there be any?

Yours, Cicely Sponge, Polegate

December 2018
Dear Mr Bar,

I had macaroni cheese for dinner last night, without the macaroni. So yes, I had cheese for dinner.

Yours, Cicely Sponge, Polegate

SPORT & LEISURE

July 2024

Dear Mr Bar,

It's a little-known fact that I was Jayne Torvill's understudy at the 1984 Winter Olympics in Sarajevo. Whilst I can't ice skate, the chemistry between Christopher Dean and me was so hot that the ice would have melted, leading to the cancellation of the Olympics and giving Jayne enough time to recover.

Yours, Cicely Sponge, Polegate

March 2024

Dear Mr Bar,

As East Croydon's Ladies Darts Quarter Finalist in 1973, I enjoyed a degree of celebrity, which opened a number of doors for me, including the VIP toilets at Cinderella Rockerfellas. Fame and recognition came at a cost though, as it wasn't long before I couldn't even go in my local Bejam. Whether this was due to my celebrity status or because I once failed to pay for a family pack of Arctic rolls, it's impossible to know.

Yours, Cicely Sponge, Polegate

January 2024

Dear Mr Bar,

I joined a gym on New Year's Day and have now cancelled my subscription. So not only have I fulfilled my resolution to join a gym, I've also saved a fortune and freed up the time I would have spent going to it.

Yours, Cicely Sponge, Polegate

July 2023
Dear Mr Bar,

If, like me, you struggle to remember the winners of Wimbledon in the 1970s, you may find the following mnemonic useful: 'Everyone likes antelopes'. Whilst none of the letters correspond to the winners' names, it is very easy to remember.

Yours, Cicely Sponge, Polegate

June 2023
Dear Mr Bar,

As Chair of Polegate's foremost Mud Wrestling and Ferret Whispering Society, we've run out of Mud. And Ferrets. Would you be interested in joining our newly formed Wrestling and Whispering Club?

Yours, Cicely Sponge, Polegate

April 2022
Dear Mr Bar,

As Chair of the Polegate & Wivelsfield Armchair Figure Skating and Fencing Society, I recently became embroiled in a heated exchange about fabric conditioners with the Chair of the Sidley & Nuneaton branch. We settled our disagreement whilst both seated and performing high-level Thrusts and Axels. I'm not saying I could negotiate world peace, but given enough armchairs, I'd be in with a shout.

Yours, Cicely Sponge, Polegate

July 2021
Dear Mr Bar,

I thought I'd let you know that having recently taken up indoor golf, I'm looking for sponsorship—and replacement windows.

Yours, Cicely Sponge, Polegate

October 2019

Dear Mr Bar,

I'm not saying a sub-two-hour marathon isn't impressive, but I once went around Croydon's IKEA quicker. Just saying.

Yours, Cicely Sponge, Polegate

October 2019

Dear Mr Bar,

As Captain of Polegate's Long Distance Snorkelling Club, I'm responsible for demisting members' goggles. The role was created after the club spent a long weekend in Jamie Oliver's hot tub, and not the Sussex Ouse as originally planned. Jamie was remarkably sanguine about it and signed almost all of our snorkels.

Yours, Cicely Sponge, Polegate

May 2019

Dear Mr Bar,

Congratulations on reaching your second anniversary. A remarkable achievement given you don't even have a bronze DofE and you perpetually split infinitives.

Yours, Cicely Sponge, Polegate

March 2019

Dear Mr Bar,

As you know, I was the first person to free climb El Capitan, an achievement I now liken to doing your 'Oojah Kappivvy'. Fewer finger holds but equally vertiginous.

Yours, Cicely Sponge, Polegate

March 2019

Dear Mr Bar,

I've just finished my first memoir entitled 'Whole Lotta Lycra'. It's about my time with Bejam's cycling team in the mid-1970s. I'd be happy to talk about it, but it's quite racy.

Yours, Cicely Sponge, Polegate

February 2019

Dear Mr Bar,

Your next show clashes with the reunion of the Totnes & Scunthorpe Bob Sleighing and Bingo Club, which club I founded in the early 1970s. It was a splinter group from the Rye & Skegness Snowboarders and Cribbage Society. We'd like to come, could you reserve us some seats?

Yours, Cicely Sponge, Polegate

January 2019
Dear Mr Bar,

During my time as a freediver in Solihull, I had a brief stint selling used ukuleles. I still have the patter and could turn it into a 15 minute 'bavard' if you'd be interested?

Yours, Cicely Sponge, Polegate

November 2018
Dear Mr Bar,

When will you have someone talking about carp fishing? Aside from fell running, it's my elderly mother's favourite pastime. However, Wednesday nights are her darts league, and she hasn't missed one in 73 years. She even gave birth to me in the snug of the Plough and Anchor so she wouldn't miss the quarter-final of the Crowhurst & Ninfield Open, completing the first-ever ladies' nine-dart finish just as her waters broke. Let me know.

Yours, Cicely Sponge, Polegate

HOBBIES & PASTIMES

September 2024
Dear Mr Bar,

As a lifelong supporter of Leamington Spa's left-handed curling team, I've only ever missed one match since the club was established in 1978. This resulted from taking a wrong turn off the B4099 and finding myself stuck behind a weekend outing of Nuneaton's Crossword and Caravanning Club. I attempted an overtaking manoeuvre but misjudged the length of a beige four-berth Elddis and inadvertently became part of the club's caravan convoy. I would have returned sooner, but it wasn't until lunchtime on the Monday that I remembered a cauliflower was a member of the brassica family, enabling me to solve seven down of the club's weekend crossword and finally exit the convoy.

Yours, Cicely Sponge, Polegate

July 2024
Dear Mr Bar,

As Chairman of Polegate's leading Submariners Association, I'm responsible for organising our annual awayday. Ideally, we'd like to spend it in a submarine, but failing that, we'd be very happy with a Wetherspoons.

Yours, Cicely Sponge, Polegate

February 2024
Dear Mr Bar,

I've just been to my antique furniture restoration group, where I met a lovely man called John. We help repair each other's antiques. As a favour, I polished his tallboy. And he's been buffing up my ormolu all afternoon.

Yours, Cicely Sponge, Polegate

September 2023
Dear Mr Bar,

As Chair of Polegate's foremost Pearl Diving Society, I would like to invite you to a taster day. We're meeting in Tesco's car park. Bring a towel. And pearls.

Yours, Cicely Sponge, Polegate

August 2023
Dear Mr Bar,

I was recently inducted into Wrexham's Penny Farthing Appreciation Society. No one was more surprised than me, as I've no interest in Penny Farthings, and I've never been to Wrexham. I feel this could be a major turning point in my life. Or a clerical error.

Yours, Cicely Sponge, Polegate

July 2023

Dear Mr Bar,

As founder member of Polegate's leading Trigonometry Society, I have a huge fondness for tangents. Do you know where I can buy a cheese grater?

Yours, Cicely Sponge, Polegate

May 2023

Dear Mr Bar,

I declined my invitation to the Coronation of HM King Charles III as it clashes with the AGM of Polegate's Advanced Underwater Cheese Thimble Bobbing Society. As you would expect, the Society is hugely popular, and as its longest-serving member (I've been underwater cheese thimble bobbing for over 50 years), it is incumbent on me to hand out the annual award of a giant cheese thimble (rough-hewn from a giant block of Canvey Island stilton) to this year's champion underwater cheese thimble bobber.

As a keen underwater cheese thimble bobber himself, (and a former recipient of a giant cheese thimble), I've no doubt HM King Charles III will fully appreciate why I am unable to attend his Coronation. To be honest, I'm a little surprised he double booked himself, not least as I'm pretty sure he'd have the 2023 underwater cheese thimble bobbing wall planner.

Yours, Cicely Sponge, Polegate

March 2023

Dear Mr Bar,

I've been asked to give my interests on a dating app. As I've aged, those interests have changed. My main interest these days is 'having an afternoon nap'. Is that appropriate?

Yours, Cicely Sponge, Polegate

October 2022

Dear Mr Bar,

As Chair of Polegate's only Vintage Thimble Club, my inbox is understandably never empty. If you could show me where the delete key is, I'd be eternally grateful.

Yours, Cicely Sponge, Polegate

September 2022

Dear Mr Bar,

As founder member of Polegate's Mountaineering & Allotment Club, I am planning on making the first known ascent up Butts Brow with a wheelbarrow full of cauliflower cheese. If you're aware of this having been done before, please let me know as I don't want to waste my time. I'm setting out at sunrise on Thursday morning.

Yours, Cicely Sponge, Polegate

September 2022

Dear Mr Bar,

I remember meeting the Queen at the anniversary breakfast of the Polegate Tuna Fishing and Hole Punching Society. As a keen Hole Puncher, the Queen was absolutely thrilled to be invited and barely complained that she had to sit on the floor as we'd run out of chairs.

Yours, Cicely Sponge, Polegate

July 2022

Dear Mr Bar,

Congratulations on reopening at Towner. Can you let Towner know I can offer them a unique exhibition of spatulas, sourced largely from Kent in the late 1970s. They could do with a bit of a rinse first though.

Yours, Cicely Sponge, Polegate

June 2022

Dear Mr Bar,

As Chairman of Polegate's Wakeboarding and Shove Ha'penny Society, I'm responsible for our annual awayday. We don't currently have any Wakeboards or Ha'pennies. Or members. So if you have any, or would like to join, please call me.

Yours, Cicely Sponge, Polegate

April 2022

Dear Mr Bar,

As founder member of Polegate's only Ice Skating and Indoor BBQ Society, I'd like to invite you to our upcoming awayday. Please wear appropriate clothing. Failing which, please wear clothing.

Yours, Cicely Sponge, Polegate

June 2020

Dear Mr Bar,

As President of Polegate's Warm to Slightly Hot Water Bathing Society, I am regularly fending off our cold water rivals. Their common claim that I'll 'feel better afterwards' belies a misunderstanding of how I presently feel, which is invariably good and never in need of a cold dunking.

Yours, Cicely Sponge, Polegate

May 2020

Dear Mr Bar,

In the early 1970s I was a founder member of the Rye & District Pebble Dashing Society. If you're looking for a bavard on the unique benefits of Pebbledashery, just ask.

Yours, Cicely Sponge, Polegate

March 2020

Dear Mr Bar,

With spring around the corner, I started thinking about working in my garden. Imagine my relief when I looked out the window and remembered I didn't have one.

Yours, Cicely Sponge, Polegate

February 2020
Dear Mr Bar,

Having recently got science, I moved on to art yesterday, and have now done that. I'll do music next week, and then that's me done. So I'll be free to dig over your vegetable patch from Wednesday onwards.

Yours, Cicely Sponge, Polegate

January 2020
Dear Mr Bar,

One of my New Year's resolutions was to become more alluring. So I've started collecting Austin Allegro Hubcaps. I haven't found any yet, so please let me know if you come across some.

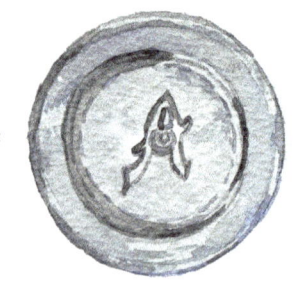

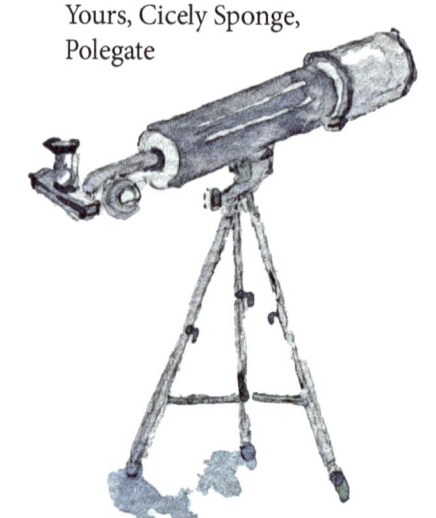

Yours, Cicely Sponge, Polegate

January 2020
Dear Mr Bar,

I have just founded the 4th East Polegate & Sidley Whale Watching Society. Observations will be held in my flat, as, on a clear day, standing on a chair and using a high-powered telescope, you can get a glimpse of the English Channel from my bathroom window. We'll post sightings on all the usual whale-watching channels.

Yours, Cicely Sponge, Polegate

November 2019

Dear Mr Bar,

Congratulations on your move to Towner. I recently offered Towner a unique opportunity to display my latest exhibition, 'Silence of the Jams', a self-curated collection of jam jars from 1983 to 1987. They declined. Their loss was Pevensey & Westham's Judo and Joinery Club's gain. Every cloud.

Yours, Cicely Sponge, Polegate

March 2019

Dear Mr Bar,

I understand your little show is having a second birthday party next week. I can't be there as it clashes with the annual dinner of the Polegate Falconry and Foliage Society. Put me down to speak at the next one, though. I'll deal with feathers, and Alfredo, my other half, will cover leaves.

Yours, Cicely Sponge, Polegate

February 2019

Dear Mr Bar,

As a former member of the Underwater Bell Ringers and Ballroom Dancers Union (I championed the merger), I have a wealth of aquatic knowledge. As well as lots of bells. I would be happy to give a demonstration at one of your shows if you'd like?

Yours, Cicely Sponge, Polegate

October 2018

Dear Mr Bar,

I went to the Bavard Bar last Wednesday and was highly disturbed. Not only did you have someone talking about 'Meteorites', a subject in which I have no interest, but no one spoke about azaleas. Why?

Yours, Cicely Sponge, Polegate

PHILOSOPHY & SPIRITUALITY

October 2024

Dear Mr Bar,

Finding myself unable to afford to pilgrimage along the Camino de Santiago, I chose instead to walk from Grantham to Worksop. What that route may lack in aesthetics was more than made up for by a plentiful supply of truck stops and roadside cafes. Plus I was able to hitch a ride for most of it, a distinct advantage over the Camino.

Yours, Cicely Sponge, Polegate

July 2024

Dear Mr Bar,

I shouldn't have listened to those people who said, 'Vote with your feet'. It's not as easy as it sounds. I made a right mess of my ballot paper.

Yours, Cicely Sponge, Polegate

May 2024

Dear Mr Bar,

According to Google, if you laid all the string in the world end to end, it would reach the moon. Which is odd, as no one knows how long a piece of string is. Makes you think, doesn't it?

Yours, Cicely Sponge, Polegate

March 2024

Dear Mr Bar,

Someone suggested I put my ducks in a row. I didn't have any ducks, so I bought some. Do you have any tips on getting them in a row?

Yours, Cicely Sponge, Polegate

February 2024

Dear Mr Bar,

Changing the subject, I was thinking to myself the other day that if I'd had a son, I'd have called him Riley. He'd live a life.

Yours, Cicely Sponge, Polegate

January 2024

Dear Mr Bar,

I recently joined Polegate's Competitive Yoga and Mindfulness Society. We were all done in a moment, leaving me free to enjoy an evening's beer and skittles down the Frog and Thistle.

Yours, Cicely Sponge, Polegate

December 2023

Dear Mr Bar,

For me, the miracle of Christmas isn't the virgin birth of a messiah. It's the notion that three men turned up, and they each brought a present.

Yours, Cicely Sponge, Polegate

October 2023

Dear Mr Bar,

As a Virgo, with Sagittarius rising, Pisces descending and a new moon in Scorpio (occasionally), I've discovered I'm fully compatible with anyone born north of the Greenwich Meridian on a Tuesday in January 1943. Provided they have their own teeth.

Yours, Cicely Sponge, Polegate

October 2023

Dear Mr Bar,

They said I'd never amount to anything. They were right. But I do have a formidable collection of linoleum offcuts.

Yours, Cicely Sponge, Polegate

August 2023

Dear Mr Bar,

According to my therapist, I 'chose' my parents. I think that's unlikely as if I had, I'd have grown up in Monaco, not Croydon.

Yours, Cicely Sponge, Polegate

April 2023

Dear Mr Bar,

Whilst cleaning my chakras last Tuesday, a pound coin fell out of my sacral chakra. Not what I was expecting, but I'm not going to look a gift horse in the mouth.

Yours, Cicely Sponge, Polegate

April 2023

Dear Mr Bar,

I decided to find myself last week, so I went to the Lake District. Whilst I can't say I became enlightened, I did become slightly damp. I'm not ruling out a connection.

Yours, Cicely Sponge, Polegate

March 2023

Dear Mr Bar,

Growing up in the '70s, we didn't have 'Helicopter Parents'. They were more like 'Space Rocket Parents'; we rarely saw them, and when we did, they generally exploded!

Yours, Cicely Sponge, Polegate

March 2023
Dear Mr Bar,

It has come to my attention that I'm ageing. I know this, as I have developed a disproportionate fondness for park benches.

Yours, Cicely Sponge, Polegate

February 2023
Dear Mr Bar,

As Secretary of Polegate's Advanced Chakra Cleansing and Bacon Grating Society, I am responsible for health & safety. From March, all members will be encouraged to wear hats, unless polishing their crown chakras. In which case hair nets are recommended.

Yours, Cicely Sponge, Polegate

December 2022
Dear Mr Bar,

If there are only 12 days of Christmas, why does it drag on for over a month?

Yours, Cicely Sponge, Polegate

September 2022
Dear Mr Bar,

As 17th in line to the Earldom of Polegate, I feel it's important to give back. So I've taken all my empty pint glasses back to the Dog & Bucket.

Yours, Cicely Sponge, Polegate

August 2022
Dear Mr Bar,

Having been mentioned in the latest Reader's Digest, my life's ambition has been fulfilled. I intend to spend the rest of my days smoking woodbines and playing the occasional game of pétanque.

Yours, Cicely Sponge, Polegate

May 2022
Dear Mr Bar,

As a trainee conspiracy theorist, I agree the Earth is flat. But what about Mars?

Yours, Cicely Sponge, Polegate (noticeably flat)

April 2022
Dear Mr Bar,

I've been to the Bavard Bar seven and a half times now, and I'm still none the wiser. Can you help?

Yours, Cicely Sponge, Polegate

March 2022
Dear Mr Bar,

Why do people want to get out of their 'comfort zone'? I've never had a comfort zone. So if you know of one, please tell me. I'd like to get in it.

Yours, Cicely Sponge, Polegate

January 2021
Dear Mr Bar,

Having survived Christmas, I need to put my bins out, and I wondered if you knew what day it is?

Yours, Cicely Sponge, Polegate

June 2020
Dear Mr Bar,

I may be late to tonight's show as, according to my Zoom online meditation and 'be here now' class, I have to spend today wrapped in vine leaves. If I can unwrap in time, I'll see you there.

Yours, Cicely Sponge, Polegate

February 2020
Dear Mr Bar,

Reading my horoscope this morning, I was astounded to learn that "finishing a job that has been complicated will fill you with pride." This has come as such a revelation to me that I've decided to finish the washing up, a job I started in June 2007.

Yours, Cicely Sponge, Polegate

January 2020
Dear Mr Bar,

I was at a loose end last Tuesday, so I decided to get science. Let me know when you've got a free speaking slot, and I'll happily bavard about it, as it's all pretty straightforward. Things do get a bit weird on the subatomic level, but I'll probably gloss over that with a bit of whistling.

Yours, Cicely Sponge, Polegate

January 2020
Dear Mr Bar,

I'll never forget the advice my old headmistress gave me on my last day of school: "Follow your dreams, Cicely. Failing which, on a cost-per-alcohol percentage basis, sherry is your best bet."

Yours, Cicely Sponge, Polegate

December 2019
Dear Mr Bar,

I've just heard that, much like the inns at the time of the Christmas story, there's no room at your December shows. Is that where the parallel ends, or can we expect a virgin birth on the night?

Yours, Cicely Sponge, Polegate

November 2019
Dear Mr Bar,

All this 'daylight time' we've been 'saving', where are we putting it?

Yours, Cicely Sponge, Polegate

October 2019
Dear Mr Bar,

I've been led to believe that life is a bit of a journey. That being so, do you know where I put my car keys?

Yours, Cicely Sponge, Polegate

September 2019
Dear Mr Bar,

As a young woman growing up in Cheam in the 1960s, life was tough. It wasn't until a Berni Inn opened on Cheam High Street in 1970 that my life started to make sense. It closed a year later, but at least I'd had a glimmer.

Yours, Cicely Sponge, Polegate

September 2019
Dear Mr Bar,

Have you ever walked into a room and forgotten why? I recently had the same experience, but in a town. Got off a coach in Skegness. No idea why. So I had some pickled herrings and came home.

Yours, Cicely Sponge, Polegate

August 2019
Dear Mr Bar,

I've just finished my 'To do' list. What now?

Yours, Cicely Sponge, Polegate

August 2019
Dear Mr Bar,

Having written the opening line of my first novella, I'm reminded of something my great aunt used to say: "Why do today what you can do tomorrow." So I'm off down the pub.

Yours, Cicely Sponge, Polegate

July 2019
Dear Mr Bar,

They say everyone has a book in them. In case you're wondering, I don't.*

Yours, Cicely Sponge, Polegate

*Fabulous Editor's note:
Things change.

July 2019
Dear Mr Bar,

At your last Bavard, there was a talk about bum reading. I have a bum and am happy for it to be read. If that helps.

Yours, Cicely Sponge, Polegate

Fabulous Editor's note:
The above pictures were drawn by Sachi Kimura-Lawson, who spoke about 'Bum Reading' at the Bavard Bar in July 2019. They came from a personalised 'trouser on' (she's not a weirdo) bum reading Sachi gave Tim B'vard. At his bum reading, the depicted characters appeared to Sachi, who explained that the woman was Tim from a previous life when he was a mid-17th-century female Russian aristocrat. The man was Tim's husband.

MUSIC

April 2024

Dear Mr Bar,

Ever since Nik Kershaw sang the immortal line, "Near a tree by a river, there's a hole in the ground", I've avoided riverside activities. You can't be too careful.

Yours, Cicely Sponge, Polegate

July 2023

Dear Mr Bar,

As Chairperson of the Sidley & Dunfermline Underwater Yodelling Society, I'd like to invite you to our annual awayday. It's being held at Lorraine Kelly's house, as she has a hot tub that can hold 50 Underwater Yodellers. If you know Lorraine, please could you ask her if it's ok to use her hot tub. And get her address.

Yours, Cicely Sponge, Polegate

May 2023
Dear Mr Bar,

I last performed at Eurovision in 1981. I wasn't booked, but I did mount the stage dressed as Huggy Bear. I made it through the first verse of "Bright Eyes" before being wrestled to the ground by a somewhat burly, if rather attractive, security chap. We dated briefly, but musical differences led to us parting company. If someone can't appreciate the raw musical genius of Bucks Fizz, they're not for me long term.

Yours, Cicely Sponge, Polegate

November 2022
Dear Mr Bar,

Touring with Howard Jones in the '80s gave me an insight into the life of a rock 'n roll superstar. It was that insight, coupled with my lack of musical ability, that led me to take up professional carp fishing. I've never looked back.

Yours, Cicely Sponge, Polegate

October 2022
Dear Mr Bar,

As President of Polegate's premier Goat Herding and Disco Club, I've organised a fundraising roller disco in the station car park. Tickets are £1.27, which entitles you to a prime organic goat burger and the choice of one track from NOW That's What I Call Music! 1985, although Level 42's "Something About You" is slightly scratched, so probably don't choose that one.

Yours, Cicely Sponge, Polegate

September 2022

Dear Mr Bar,

As the little-known sixth member of the Spice Girls, I rarely get the recognition I deserve. But without me, there would have been no "Zig-a-Zig-Ah", and a band without "Zig-a-Zig-Ah" is like a stew without turnips. That's right Mr Bar, I was the Spice Girls' missing turnip.

Yours, Cicely Sponge, Polegate

June 2022

Dear Mr Bar,

Congratulations on your fifth anniversary. I also recently celebrated an anniversary. It's been five years since I started playing the Tuba, and not a day goes by when you can't hear me belting out "Dancing Queen" to the happy amusement of the local townsfolk.

Yours, Cicely Sponge, Polegate

January 2022

Dear Mr Bar,

I've refined my New Year's resolutions. Rather than becoming trilingual, I've decided to learn to play the cymbals.

Yours, Cicely Sponge, Polegate

November 2021

Dear Mr Bar,

I've just returned from a tour of Suffolk with Jennifer Aniston and her Nasal Accordion. Credit for the success of the tour should, of course, go to Ms Aniston. However, I must point out that our near-sold-out gig at Pontins in Lowestoft would have been a complete failure had I not been there to improvise on bass triangle and washboard.

Yours, Cicely Sponge, Polegate

September 2021

Dear Mr Bar,

I've just returned from a tour of Peckham with William Shatner's Washboard and Harmonica Ensemble. If you haven't heard Shatner tear up the Prodigy's "Firestarter" on a 1950s Columbus washboard, you haven't lived.

Yours, Cicely Sponge, Polegate

February 2020

Dear Mr Bar,

I recently pulled out all the stops. I'd be grateful for your help as I really need to put them back.

Yours, Cicely Sponge, Polegate

January 2020

Dear Mr Bar,

I'd like to apologise to anyone who witnessed my behaviour on Sunday afternoon. I'd had a little too much Bristol Cream at the annual lunch of Polegate's Tapas and Tapestry Club. Suffice to say, no one needed to hear my rendition of "Livin La Vida Loca". Nor did they need to see me perform it wearing just a hi-vis and sombrero.

Yours, Cicely Sponge, Polegate

November 2019

Dear Mr Bar,

I heard that Bublé today crooning about things "beginning to look a lot like Christmas." Well, unless Christmas resembles a pair of marigolds and an armful of antifoul, not from where I'm standing.

Yours, Cicely Sponge, Polegate

November 2019

Dear Mr Bar,

Apparently, "It's a long way to Tipperary." Maybe, but not if you live in Cork.

Yours, Cicely Sponge, Polegate

October 2019

Dear Mr Bar,

In the mid-1960s, at the height of my skiffle career with 'Cicely and her Sponges', I played the Whitby Empire. It was a rainy night in November, with a wind chill that could freeze sprouts in an Aga, but the crowd that showed up were stoic—and surprised. Never give up, Mr Bar. I didn't, despite repeated requests.

Yours, Cicely Sponge, Polegate

October 2019

Dear Mr Bar,

People, including Enya, often ask me what my inspiration was for "Orinoco Flow". In the mid 1980s I managed a plumber's merchant in Wimbledon. It wrote itself.

Yours, Cicely Sponge, Polegate

October 2019
Dear Mr Bar,

I consoled myself for missing out on Glastonbury tickets by remembering that I really like sleeping in a house.

Yours, Cicely Sponge, Polegate

September 2019
Dear Mr Bar,

"Are you going to Scarborough Fair?" is a good question with a limited number of answers, including yes, no, or maybe. "Parsley, sage, rosemary and thyme" seems a bit left field. Could you shed any light?

Yours, Cicely Sponge, Polegate

May 2019
Dear Mr Bar,

As a former Eurovision contestant, I have a number of stories of backstage shenanigans involving myself, Mr Wogan, three members of Bucks Fizz and the Copenhagen ice hockey team. For a pickled egg and pint of mild, I'll tell all at your anniversary show. Let me know.

Yours, Cicely Sponge, Polegate

April 2019
Dear Mr Bar,

On reflection, making Kate Bush's "Greatest Hits" the only album I took to my desert island was a mistake. I'm not saying there aren't some classics on there, but 28 years of "Babooshka" has left me as weak as a kitten.

Yours, Cicely Sponge, Polegate

December 2018

Dear Mr Bar,

I may be late to Wednesday's Bavard Bar as I've just returned from a tour of Finland with Sylvester Stallone's 'Magical Recorder Band' and am nursing a hangover following an end-of-tour game of Twister. 'What goes on tour stays on tour', but suffice to say Mr Stallone is incredibly flexible for a man of his years.

Yours, Cicely Sponge, Polegate

December 2018

Dear Mr Bar,

Is there any truth in the rumour that you repaired Mick Jagger's tumble dryer in the late 1970s? Only mine's just stopped working.

Yours, Cicely Sponge, Polegate

December 2018

Dear Mr Bar,

Following yesterday's rumour that you were Mick Jagger's original tumble dryer repair man, is there any truth in the internet rumour that the Spice Girls' lyrical masterpiece, "Wannabe", was inspired by you? I only ask as I have the original "Spice" album and wondered if you would sign it for me.

Yours, Cicely Sponge, Polegate

WORK & MONEY

September 2023
Dear Mr Bar,

I come from a long line of Sponges, going back to 1066 when my family, the Sponges of Limoges, fought alongside William the Conqueror at Hastings. My ancestor, Cecil de Sponge de Limoges, was William's mobile hairdresser. He was single-handedly responsible for ensuring William's trademark side parting was never out of place, even when skirmishing.

Yours, Cicely Sponge, Polegate

July 2023
Dear Mr Bar,

After spending the weekend with Prince William, I've decided to turn my back on the nine-to-five and become a Monarch. If you know of any openings or countries that require ruling, please let me know.

Yours, Cicely Sponge, Polegate

June 2022
Dear Mr Bar,

I finished all the books yesterday. So if you've any jobs that need doing, I'm available.

Yours, Cicely Sponge, Polegate

October 2021
Dear Mr Bar,

Is it possible to pay for petrol in instalments?

Yours, Cicely Sponge, Polegate

April 2020
Dear Mr Bar,

Imagine my surprise when I rolled out of bed this morning to find myself immediately at work. I don't even have a job.

Yours, Cicely Sponge, Polegate

February 2020

Dear Mr Bar,

I've decided to identify as an A-list millionaire supermodel. If I'm a bit wrinkly when I see you, it's because I intend to spend the next month in my bath. Which I've identified as a yacht.

Yours, Cicely Sponge,
Polegate

January 2020

Dear Mr Bar,

I've decided to work towards financial independence. Any chance you could see your way to giving me tax free regular income, free housing and unlimited travel to ease the transition?

Yours, Cicely Sponge, Polegate

September 2019

Dear Mr Bar,

I noticed recently that you claimed to have been double glazing windows since records began. When, exactly, did records begin?

Yours, Cicely Sponge, Polegate

September 2019
Dear Mr Bar,

I recently attended a conference on the persistent use of workshops at conferences. In my workshop, we also considered the persistent use of conferences. Overall, I would have preferred a blue biro, but the mints were great.

Yours, Cicely Sponge, Polegate

July 2019
Dear Mr Bar,

Whilst I wasn't the first person on the moon, I was the first person to use bullet points in East Sussex—a not inconsiderable achievement when you consider a world without such a grammatical system.

Yours, Cicely Sponge, Polegate

June 2019
Dear Mr Bar,

I've just cashed in my nectar points from the past 20 years. I didn't need a desk tidy, but I'm not going to look a gift horse in the mouth.

Yours, Cicely Sponge, Polegate

Fabulous Editor's note:
I was unsure about Tim's choice of illustration at the end of the book. Then I remembered, "It's all nonsense". So I put it in.

ACKNOWLEDGEMENTS

As with many projects, this book is more than the efforts of just one person.

It is unlikely to have ever seen the light of day if it weren't for the tireless efforts of my fabulous editor, Laurine Waille. Knowing how delightfully incapable I have become of applying myself to detail, Laurine quietly ensured that tasks I see as tedious and would run miles to avoid became fun-filled instead. I'd also like to thank Julia Chi Taylor for so lovingly enjoying Cicely's nonsense and sending unsolicited positive and joyful messages to me, after reading many of them. In the same vein, I'd like to thank Athena Jane Churchill, Susie Barnard and Karen Reid for telling me often, and again unsolicited, how much they enjoyed Cicely's observations. Over the years, I have received numerous messages from people telling me how they nearly spat out their coffee while reading Cicely's latest musings over breakfast. If you were one of those people, then I apologise for the wasted coffee, but thank you from the bottom of my heart, as it is in part due to your messages that I was inspired to continue.

I would like to thank my daughter, Hannah, for coming up with the name 'Bavard Bar'. Had she not come with me to meet Chris Berry at Printers Playhouse in February 2017, and had she not been revising for her French GCSE at the time, who knows what the show would have been called. And without the support of the venues where the Bavard Bar is performed every month, Cicely is again very unlikely to have emerged, there being no foil for her correspondence. So to that end, I would like to extend enormous thanks to Kino-Teatr and, in particular, the tireless efforts of Olga Mamanova, Russell Baker and Simon Charterton in ensuring St Leonards and Hastings has one of the country's finest arts venues in the form of Kino-Teatr. Likewise to the contemporary powerhouse that is Towner in Eastbourne and the support of Joe Hill, Niamh Pearce, Hannah Jordan and Davey Strange. Not to mention the wonderful Berry family and Printers Playhouse in Eastbourne, where the show began in March 2017.

Thanks must also go to the hundreds of fabulous bavarders who have trodden the boards to share their stories at the Bavard Bar month after month. They have delighted, surprised, intrigued, amused, and, above all, entertained countless people. Along with those brave and possibly foolhardy souls who have stepped up to play one of my bonkers wild card comedy games.

Added to which, I would like to thank the wonderful audiences of those South Coast towns and beyond, who have turned up en masse, month after month, selling out the venues, listening to my nonsense and enjoying the sometimes incredible, often eclectic, always extraordinary, stories of regular folk who have turned bavarders for the night. Many audience members have come month after month, some from the beginning, and to all of the audiences, whether they have returned or not, I offer my deepest thanks.

There is then the team behind the Bavard Bar, all of whom help create what audience members have described as often 'magical' and occasionally 'unforgettable' nights. To Piano Man Dan for being in at the start and uniquely arranging and playing songs linked to the night's bavards, however obscurely. To Maria O'Neill, for again being with me from near the beginning, turning up month after month to draw and paint the bavarders in the most awkward and dimly lit of artists' studios imaginable, and of course, for providing the beautiful illustrations that lift this book into something significantly more than just a compilation of nonsensical letters. And to the most recent member of the team, Marky Sparky, whose extraordinary technical talents appear to know no bounds and who has elevated the show, at times, to a surprisingly professional level. Marky also helped Cicely write one of her letters.

There are, of course, many others who deserve thanks but whom I have inadvertently forgotten. Please be assured that I mean no disrespect, and please accept my heartfelt thanks if I have overlooked naming you in these acknowledgements.

ABOUT THE AUTHOR

I grew up in the suburbs of South London in the 1970s and '80s. Aside from my mum's delicious home cooking, I was sustained by a diet of Findus Crispy Pancakes and Sodastream and enjoyed a lifestyle that ensured my always bare knees were near permanently grazed. Somehow surviving, despite a welcome lack of health and safety guidance, barely any warning signs and no mobile communication methods other than string-connected tin cans, I miraculously lived to pursue a career in the legal profession and qualified as a Solicitor in the City of London in the 1990s. After a short stint in the City post-qualification, I practised provincially for a brief period before setting up my own law firm. My firm developed a strong national reputation within its niche sector such that I was elected to serve on the Law Society Council for my specialism.

To escape from the stresses of running a busy law firm, practising as a lawyer in courtrooms across the country, speaking at legal conferences and being a Law Society Council member, I ran—a lot. And as often as I could, I ran in the North Western fells of England.

The other thing I did was go to a small underground basement speaking club in the back streets of Brighton called the Catalyst Club. Hosted by David Bramwell, the premise of the club, inspired by the culture of French Salons and Speakeasies, was three people talking about something they loved for about 15 minutes each. David had been running the club since 2004, and I was so inspired by the talks that one night, I spoke at his club and shared my passion for fell running, in particular the (to me) legendary Lakeland Bob Graham Round. That was 2016.

Not long after, I set up my own version of a speaking club. I called it the Bavard Bar. The name was inspired by my then 16-year-old daughter, Hannah. She was revising for her French GCSE at the time, and whilst telling her about my idea and looking for a name, she told me that the French verb 'bavarder' means 'to chat'. The word 'bar' was an obvious alliterative addition, and gave a nod to my legal background as well as giving hope to the drinking proclivities of my, as yet unmet, audience.

Thanks, in part, to the patience and understanding of my former business partner, Julie Allen, the show grew over the years and now involves many more elements than a regular speaking night or club. Those additional elements have come from my love of nonsensical and absurdist comedy and humour, and to my delight, the audiences have loved these additions, and so the audience has developed and grown with the show.

Having sold my law firm in 2021, and aside from still running a lot, I now spend most of my time hosting the Bavard Bar and MCing comedy nights and other shows and events when asked.

bavardbar.co.uk

ABOUT THE ARTIST

Maria O'Neill is an artist living and working in St Leonards-on-Sea since 2016.

Born in Ireland, Maria has painted all her life. As well as East Sussex, Maria has lived in Malawi, Bahrain and West London, depicting life around her in her paintings in all those places.

Maria's current home town of St Leonards offers her bountiful scope for paintings, with its seaside lifestyle and delightfully quirky characters she loves to include in her paintings.